My business book of the year.

PHIL JESSON

This is a book that is packed with insights for today's world. It deals with the reality of where our world is today and gives you solid, usable actions, not a bunch of "feel good" ideas.

TERRY L., BROCK, MARKETING COACH & AUTHOR, USA

As the COO of a company with technology, intelligent solutions and global expansion at the heart of our strategy, this book was written just for us. I will be ordering a copy for all our people as this will be the way to do business.

LIZZ MUNDAY, COO, IQARUS

Another brilliant book from the master of concise, common sense but invaluable business advice.

ANDREW KLUGE, CEO, COSATTO

Overall, you can't go wrong with this book by your side. Not only will you discover how to ensure your business is a winner, but you will also be able to explore a wealth of additional information to help you succeed.

G. JONES, INTERNET PSYCHOLOGIST AND LECTURER

Informative, to the point, practical advice. Excellent read, lots of food for thought. I recommend it for all CEOs, branch managers, line managers, current and prospective business owners, and companies that would like to expand.

JACQUES VAN NIEKERK, CTO, SOUTH AFRICA

WIN!

How to succeed in the new game of business

ROGER HARROP
JUANITA VORSTER

Publisher: The CEO Experts™
Website: www.theceoexperts.com

1st Edition authored by Roger Harrop, published in 2014 by SRA Books and reprinted in 2015 and 2016.
Paperback ISBN 978-1-909116-38-2
Ebook eISBN 978-1-909116-39-9

2nd Edition authored by Juanita Vorster and Roger Harrop, published in 2020.
Paperback ISBN 978-0-620-90052-2
Ebook eISBN 978-0-620-90053-9

App developer: Ralph Harris

Editing: Lizann Keuler
Cover design: Juanita Vorster
Typesetting: Liezl Strydom

Print on demand
Printing and binding by:
Groep 7 Drukkers en Uitgewers (Pty) Ltd
Pretoria, www.groep7.co.za

Roger's thanks to:
Christine LeHeup

Juanita's thanks to:
My family for unconditional support.
Roger (for allowing me to meddle).

CONTENTS

SECOND EDITION NOTES

IN THE YEARS before the first edition of this book, business was struggling to grasp the new game of business created by technological disruption.

The 2020 COVID-19 pandemic changed the game once again and triggered the second edition of this book. This edition adds updated information and stories to the winning strategy described in the first edition.

This book is the ideal quick reference guide for anyone running – or involved in running – any business. Now all you need is a fire in your belly and a sparkle in your eye to WIN! in the new game of business!

THE STORY BEHIND

THE

CEO EXPERTS™

DURING ONE OF Roger's masterclasses a delegate came up to him during a break and said: 'Roger, you really are the CEO expert, aren't you?'

The moniker stuck, and Roger started using it as part of his branding.

Fast forward to 2019 when we – Juanita, based in South Africa, and Roger, based in the UK – happened to meet at a conference in South Africa.

As we chatted, we discovered that we both had the same reason for being professional speakers: we want to make success easier for business leaders and we want to keep it simple.

So it made sense that we combine our strengths. Since then Juanita – as 'The Next CEO Expert' – adds an updated flair to Roger's wisdom that has already helped over 30 000 business leaders in over 50 countries.

For more information or to book Roger or Juanita for a keynote, seminar, masterclass, strategic planning event or to discuss consultancy advice visit **www.theceoexperts.com.**

ABOUT ROGER – THE ORIGINAL CEO EXPERT

Roger Harrop BSc(Hons), CEng, FIMechE, FCIM, FInstIB, FPSA, PSAE, CSPGlobal

Roger Harrop has spent over 25 years leading international businesses, including a Public Limited Company (PLC), which puts him in a unique position to deal with present-day business challenges.

Based in Oxford in the UK, he's an international business growth speaker who inspires and entertains audiences with his acclaimed *Staying in the Helicopter*® programmes. Over 30 000 CEOs, business leaders and others, across 50 countries, have achieved transformational change through his thought-provoking and entertaining talks laced with real-life stories and humour.

Roger is also an author, business advisor, mentor, consultant and independent director.

He has unusually wide leadership experience: from small start-ups to multi-nationals and from high-tech products to basic commodities, people-based service businesses and not-for-profit organisations.

Roger spent seven years as Group Chief Executive of a FTSE quoted, high-tech industrial group with 12 sites across four continents. The UK Government mentioned it in its 'Competitiveness' White Paper. Forbes Magazine in the US included the group among its list of the top 100 overseas companies. Two business schools have used it as a benchmark case study on culture change and business re-engineering.

Roger tutored on a leading leadership and teambuilding programme for over 25 years.

He's a keen mountain biker and classic car enthusiast.

www.rogerharrop.com

ABOUT JUANITA – THE NEXT CEO EXPERT

Juanita Vorster Cert.Dir, EO

Juanita Vorster is a successful entrepreneur with a knack for turning complex business concepts into simplified, practical advice. She also holds the designations of Certified Director and Ethics Officer.

As an 'old millennial' she has experienced the world of work how it used to be as well as where it has shifted to.

Juanita founded her own fully remote working and highly regarded outsourced marketing business in 2013. The company has reported profitable growth every year since its inception with very low churn in staff and clients. She is still very much involved in running her company and uses the lessons she learns from it to keep her advice and stories practical and fresh.

Based in South Africa, Juanita is also an international speaker, author of a number of articles in highly respected publications, a regular guest on business podcasts and a former radio programme host.

www.juanitavorster.com

A LETTER FROM US TO YOU

DEAR BUSINESS LEADER,

If you are to be not just a winner but a serial winner in this new game of business, then you need three things above all else. And they are all heart things, not head things.

Belief, Passion and Courage.

As a business leader, you've got to believe. You have to believe in whatever it is you're doing. If you don't believe, you'll get found out by your employees, by your financiers and your customers. If you don't truly believe in what you're doing, don't do it.

You also have to lead with passion. Passion is not something you should leave at home. It should ooze out of the pores of your skin. Passion is infectious. People follow people with passion – it's what they need to see from you everywhere and every day.

Finally, you need courage. Businesses only move forward if you take risks. That's what your job is as a business leader – to take risks and make tough decisions. Maybe we even have to take a few more risks than we used to. Whether it's the risk of setting the highest standards for your people, putting your prices up by a per cent or two tomorrow, or the risk of trying out a new market or technology – if you have the courage to relentlessly focus on the four fundamentals of business in this book, we guarantee you will WIN!

BEFORE YOU READ ANY FURTHER ...

It may not look like it, but you're holding in your hand a high-tech book with access to videos, white papers, animations, interactive business assessments and more!

We've added everything to help you WIN! in this new game of business.

So how do you maximise the winning value of this book?

First, make sure your smartphone can read the QR codes included throughout the book. For newer model smartphones, it is as easy as opening the camera app and pointing at the QR code.

If your smartphone doesn't have a QR code reader embedded, you can download a free QR code reader from your phone's app store:

- QuickScan
- RedLaser
- ScanLife

The app contains a few business assessments that will help you to immediately apply what you learn in your own business.

Use the app regularly so you can view the progress of your business over time. That way you can make sure you really are winning!

Now, scan the QR code below to access and use this book's app.

THE STATE OF PLAY

BUSINESS HAS NEVER been more interesting, challenging or rewarding.

Winning in business is not reserved for the elite few who run multi-national corporations.

The range of technology available these days has revolutionised the way business operates. It has also created the threat of being left behind by those that are better at adapting to this new game of business.

The playing field of business is increasingly being levelled – a bright idea and an internet connection seems to be the only thing you need to start the next big thing. No business leader can afford to ignore technological advances and the societal shifts it brings.

Whatever they're selling and wherever they are in the world, we're seeing some small and medium enterprises run rings around many big corporations. They often do it by swiftly adopting the latest innovations in technology in a way that larger companies can find difficult.

The winners in this new game are those that can see through the noise and keep it simple, because business at its core is simple.

Someone wants to buy, someone wants to sell, and in the middle, someone needs to make a product or offer a service. That's it.

Top scorers don't make excuses. They play to win. Playing without striving to win is not an option for them.

Nor should it be in business.

Without growth, business is dead in the water. A business should not just exist. It needs to continuously adapt and grow. The only alternative is to stagnate and, sooner or later, die.

Business owners and business leaders have to regularly get up in the helicopter and spend time looking at the big picture in order to make business growth happen.

When we deliver masterclasses to business owners and leaders, we ask them: 'What is holding you back? Why aren't you going or growing as fast as you'd like?'

The answers we get are generally:

- My team is resistant to change
- I have trouble finding and keeping talent
- It's the economic crisis
- Banks won't lend
- I can't get investment
- I struggle to find the time for business development
- My people aren't selling
- It's the changing markets
- I have no plan; I just wing it
- We operate in a risk averse culture
- No one wants to spend money

See our book Staying in the Helicopter®: The Key to Sustained Profitable Growth

> During a WIN! masterclass one delegate CEO said: 'I've just realised something about all these issues we put on the flip chart this morning... None of them are real, are they? I mean, in actual fact, they are just excuses, aren't they? The reason we're not growing as fast as I would like is me. Nothing else!'

What excuses have you been making and what are you allowing to get in the way of your business winning this new game?

The companies that are really flying right now are those that know how to focus on the fundamentals of business. It doesn't matter what sector they're in, whether they operate for profit or not, what size they are, or where they are in the world; when a company focuses on the four fundamentals of business it really can't fail.

In this book we show you how you too can succeed by focusing on the fundamentals of the new game of business:

- Win! By being exceptional
- Win! By being a great place to work... and play
- Win! By constantly prospecting
- Win! By focusing on the score – the triple bottom line

FUNDAMENTAL ONE

WIN! BY BEING EXCEPTIONAL

It's no longer about being good enough at what you do. Quite simply, you have to be absolutely exceptional at everything you do any time and anywhere you do it.

NEVER BE AFRAID OF THE COMPETITION

Thanks to the shrinking of the world through technological advances, a small company can now run circles around much bigger businesses. The sky really is the limit, no matter what size of organisation you are and where you are in the world.

In the corporate world people – mostly finance people – are forever talking about 'industry averages'. Average margins, average prices, average effort.

There is no way to win the new game of business by being average or even by being just a bit better than average.

To win, a business has to first and foremost be absolutely exceptional at what it does.

Frankly, if your business or its products or services are mediocre, you're finished. Or you're about to be.

Take a look for a moment at what you sell. If you are really objective about it, what do you see? Is it actually pretty much the same as everyone else's? Maybe a little better or a little worse? Essentially, it's probably much the same.

So how can you take the lead in a world where so many are doing or making the same thing? How can you differentiate yourself from the competition?

We are fascinated by giant killers: people who have taken on the biggest in the world and won.

> In 1979, the now-famous home appliances company Dyson was started by James Dyson, a British engineer who got fed up with the inefficiency of his vacuum cleaner.
>
> Unable to sell his revolutionary design to UK-based home appliance manufacturers he tried licensing it in the US through Amway, once again with no luck. So he borrowed almost a million pounds and became a manufacturer himself. It took 15 years from when he first had the idea to when his vacuum cleaner became the best-seller in the world.
>
> Nowadays, Dyson is known for reinventing home appliances that everybody sees as being at the end of the development lifecycle and not worth investing in – and selling it at prices much higher than the market average. A Dyson hairdryer was once the most sought-after Christmas gift in the UK, and it flew off the shelves, even though it was six times the price of the competition!

Read the article How I Did It: James Dyson

Exceptional companies don't set their aspirations by looking back at the competition. They don't accept industry norms.

Exceptional companies set their own standards.

Just imagine, if James Dyson had gone to a top consulting firm for advice to launch his first vacuum cleaner, what would those consultants have said in return for their big fat fee? 'It's just a vacuum cleaner; set your prices just below that of the most popular competitor model.'

Dyson shows us we should never be frightened of the competition. Never get into the mindset of 'We may never be Number 1.' If you think like that, all you'll ever be is Number 2. You and your business can do anything. It's up to you. There are so many examples these days of organisations that went from nothing to dominating the world and doing it incredibly quickly.

We can all do it. It is only us that limit our potential to grow.

In a race, we know that if you're in the lead and you spend too much time looking back at those following you, your competitors will more easily close the gap between you and them.

Run your own race, play your own game and set your own strategy – not theirs – to win.

ADAPT TO THE NEW MARKET DYNAMIC

Increasingly, we are seeing that the way by which exceptional organisations differentiate themselves from the competition is the process through which they take their customers.

Product/Process Matrix

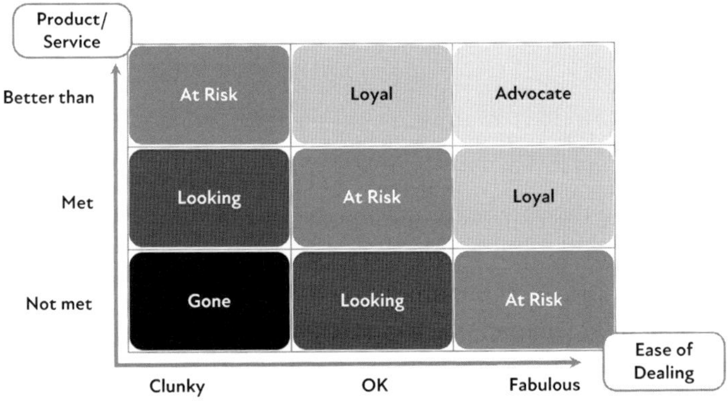

On the Y axis is the status of your product or service in terms of meeting the expectations of your customers: not met, met, or better than expected.

On the X axis is the process through which your customers have to go to buy your product or service. Is it clunky, OK or absolutely fabulous?

Imagine you read an article about a new restaurant in town and you decide to try them out. They serve you some of the best food you've ever had, but it takes two hours to come to the table. How likely are you to recommend the restaurant to a friend? And how likely are you to go back?

You need to have every one of your customers in the three boxes in the top right corner. Brand advocates and loyalists become an unpaid sales force. They are so delighted by how easy it is to deal with your company and how great your product or service is that they spread the word to others they know will want the same experience.

Any customer that is in any other block in this product/process matrix is either at risk of going to your competitor, already looking at alternative options or already gone.

And there's something else – in our experience there's another dimension to this new dynamic.

You need to pay at least as much attention to designing the customer experience as you do to designing products and services. Often even more.

CREATE A MEMORABLE EXPERIENCE

Customer experience (CX) can add massive value to what you're doing.

Think about how Lego has used this to their advantage. Fans can create memories with their favourite toy at home, with friends, online, at an amusement park and in movie theatres. Lego is not just a plastic brick manufacturer, it's a whole experience!

Great customer experience isn't just something that happens – you've got to design it. To grow brand advocates, your customer experience must be differentiating, influential, valuable and consistent.

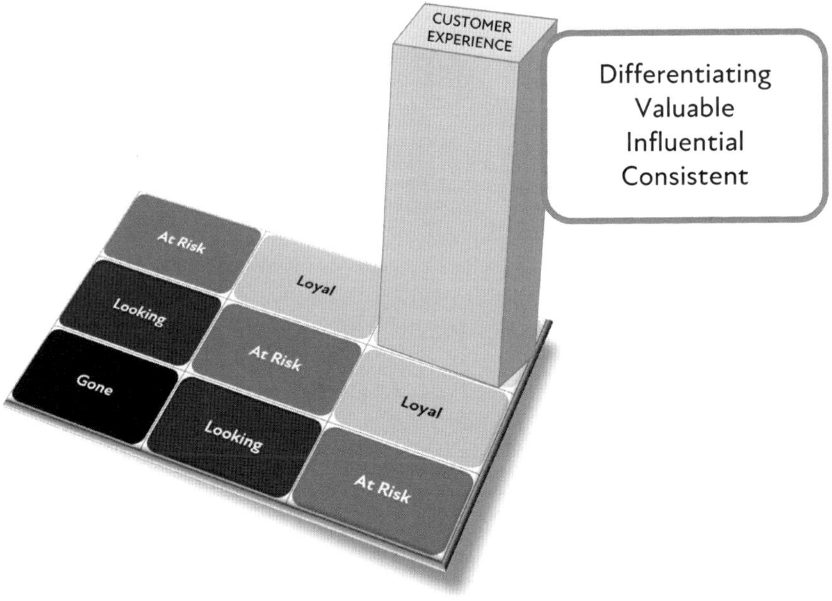

Differentiating

Even if what you sell is a commodity or exactly the same as your competitors, the way your staff treat people when they sell your products to customers can make an even bigger difference. There's still a lot of value in showing good manners and serving with a smile.

It's possible to go even further than basic good service. A free gift with every purchase or easy loyalty programme can be all it takes.

I frequent a butchery that isn't on my regular route of errands. The quality and prices of the meat are the same as elsewhere, but the service is more personal. Also, every time I go in with my children they leave with a free piece of biltong!

This small gesture of handing out a free piece of a South African delicacy surely doesn't cost the butchery much, but it attracts families who need to get the shopping done while keeping kids happy.

Juanita

Valuable

Customers don't just want to buy products and services – they want to feel understood and taken care of when they deal with you.

Are your customer-facing employees giving customers their full attention and making sure they have everything they need? Or are they chatting with colleagues, checking their phones, and generally just waiting for their shift to end?

Are your people that render your services always doing everything to the best of their ability, making sure at every step that the customer is kept informed, and following up with an after-sales check-in call?

Influential

You've got to treat customers in a way that will make them want to share their experience with family, friends, colleagues and on social media. People will share their experiences anyway, so make sure what they share is what you want them to share. And if you see that they've shared their experience online, respond to them!

Consistent

Having got all that sorted, make sure that the customer has the same great experience every single time they deal with your brand, wherever that is. This is difficult to do across remote locations or when you work with supplier partners, but it's your responsibility to make sure everyone understands 'how we treat customers around here'.

Creating incredible customer experiences isn't just for large companies with big budgets – small businesses have as much opportunity to delight their customers.

I had an appointment to see the owner of a jewellery shop in a really deprived area. As I arrived there was a parade of shops, with the jewellers in the middle and a charity shop on each side.

I remember thinking 'I'm not sure what I'm going to be able to do here'. As I got to the front of the shop, I saw that there was no door to open. I had to press a button, and it was like an airlock opening! The door closed behind me and after a two second delay the next 'airlock' door opened in front.

Standing in the open door was an assistant – impeccably dressed – with a glass of champagne at the ready. They do this for every single customer.

It was like going to another planet. Everything was immaculate – beautiful carpeting, stainless steel everywhere, with probably twice as many assistants as anywhere else. Every single one was an expert in specific types of jewellery, and they encouraged you to stay there as long as you like.

This jewellery chain – with only two shops – now sells no watches for under £3 500 and they are the biggest customer in Europe for a particular brand of Swiss watch.

Everyone who goes into that shop knows that every single thing they're buying is available online, probably at half the price. But people come from all over the UK to go to those shops – because of the experience.

Roger

That's the world we are living in now. Giving 100% is no longer good enough. Every time and everywhere you deal with a client or customer you have to be giving at least 110%.

Exceptional companies set their own rules. They decide what they are going to achieve, where they are going to go, and how they're going to get there. They do it in a way that exceeds all industry averages and customer expectations.

And they use technology to help them do it.

This is* your *responsibility. You can't afford to leave tech to the techies. So don't skip the next section!

DEVELOP A NEW CORE COMPETENCE

To be truly exceptional, every business needs a new core competence: the assimilation, adaptation and adoption of new technology – which is arriving at eye-watering speed.

None of us can afford to ignore it.

New Core Competence

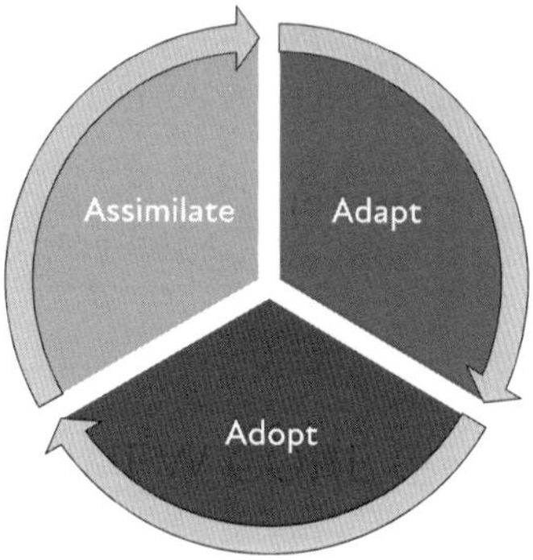

You might think that all new technology is expensive, or that it is only accessible to those that have a technology qualification. Technology these days can be used by anyone in any business that chooses to embrace it.

We must not assume where a technology might find use in our organisation – don't let it disappear into a silo – it just might find use anywhere.

You've got to know about more technology than just your core operating systems. If the smart use of technology isn't happening throughout your organisation right now, then you need to make sure it starts happening tomorrow.

The Hut Group, based in Manchester, UK, employs 5 500 people rising to 10 000, sells in 164 countries and is valued at £5.5 billion. That's larger than Marks & Spencer.

THG sells health and beauty products through 166 websites and owns brands such as Myprotein, ESPA and Mankind and has developed technology that allows its customers to shop on their phones and receive orders the next day.

Matthew Moulding, the co-founder and CEO, runs this entire corporation through his iPhone where he has a dashboard that keeps him up to date with the entire business in real time.

I run my company entirely in the cloud. I only use software that can be operated online as opposed to software that needs to be installed on a computer. This setup supports the fully remote-working structure that I created back in 2011.

In this structure anyone can work together on projects from anywhere on almost any device. Managers have full oversight of all key performance areas at all times, and the handover of projects during leave periods are glitch-free.

Best of all? None the software and apps I use are very expensive. Some are even completely free to use.

Juanita

You don't need to know how all the available technology works; you just need to know that it's there and what it can do for your business.

So let's look at some technology examples:

Take 3D printing. Now, 3D printing is not new. In fact, it's been around for more than three decades and yet it's only recently that people have started to talk about it as potentially having the same impact on the world as the first Industrial Revolution.

It was called 'rapid prototyping' by engineers and it stayed with them until recently, when it started to be used to its full potential in other areas. We must never 'lose' technology like that again – technology might find use anywhere in our organisation

There are amazing technical things that can be done by 3D printing, such as titanium parts for satellites and aircrafts. An increasing amount of replacement body parts are now being 3D printed and since the setup costs are so little it means your new knee could be made unique to you to better mimic your own joint when it was healthy.

3D printing

3D printing is also being used far more creatively in all kinds of applications and areas of the organisation. From printing personalised promotional items and gifts, to printing custom shoes, buildings and even food – the application of 3D printing has broken out of the engineering silo.

4D printing

4D, 5D and now 6D printing are 3D printing's even more exciting new siblings and hold lots of amazing potential.

Scan the QR codes to watch videos about *3D printing body parts, 4D printing self-assembling furniture, and 6D printing.*

6D printing

QR codes are another example of something that is incredibly simple to make and use. The main function of a QR code is to be a simple bridge between the offline (printed) and online worlds. That's what you've hopefully been doing so far by reading this book and accessing the additional videos and downloads through the codes.

QR codes are most often used by sales and marketing departments, but they have also been cleverly adopted for many other uses.

The South African platform uKeshe uses QR codes to enable digital payments to informal traders, street vendors and casual labourers who don't have bank accounts or can't afford traditional point of sale devices.

A few years ago, I got a new knee in hospital. My identity bracelet didn't have my name on it; it had a QR code that linked to all my medical records. Every time any procedure was done the medical personnel scanned the QR code on my bracelet and had immediate access to everything they needed to know.

Roger

In Japan, dementia patients get a QR code glued to their thumbnails every three weeks. If they get lost or forget where they are, anyone with a smartphone can scan the QR code and help them back to where they can be taken care of.

Who's thinking like this in your organisation!?

Augmented Reality (AR) is a bit more complex to implement but is gaining popularity very fast. Not too long ago, AR seemed to be more at home in science fiction movies than in business. AR has, however, become increasingly valuable in training, events, retail, tourism, design and even agriculture.

Have a look at the best AR marketing experiences

At an agriculture conference where I was a keynote speaker, I saw a demonstration on how Augmented Reality is used on dairy farms.

Each cow wears a tag that is picked up by a scanner operated by the farmer. When pointed at a cow the display of the scanner shows all the information about the cow; from identifying number to the amount of feed consumed to the amount of milk produced.

The integrated software tracks the data from every cow and alerts the farmer if there are signs of illness or any other issues that need attention. This makes it much easier for a farmer to make quick, informed decisions that can have a massive impact on the income of the farm.

Juanita

Have you ever considered how you can make use of augmented reality in your business?

We can't have a chapter on technology in this book without touching on Artificial Intelligence (AI). This often-misunderstood technology can help any business increase sales, reduce costs, keep employees engaged and keep customers happy.

Read about the Nuru app

AI can process enormous amounts of raw data into usable information in a fraction of the time that humans can. It does this by running data through a set of rules. This process translates the data into insights to help us make informed decisions quicker. In an automated facility, these insights trigger machine activity to optimise operations.

The AI-driven Nuru app is used by farmers in Africa to increase the yield of their crops by up to 50% by helping them to diagnose plant diseases. Nuru was developed by Penn State University.

The app allows the farmers to take a photo of an ailing plant. The photo is then matched with an offline database of plant diseases. Once an online connection is available, the app links to the PlantVillage platform managed by the app developers. This connection allows the farmers to receive bespoke advice from government and academic experts in a range of local languages.

The big debate at the time of writing this book was how many and what types of jobs AI will replace. The other side of the debate struggles with how a completely human workforce can compete against an artificial intelligence workforce.

Our advice is that you learn enough about AI so that you can decide what you want it to do for you, not the other way around. It is completely possible for human intelligence and artificial intelligence to work together – and it starts with you deciding what that will look like for your business.

It is clear that technology is not just for the technical side of any business. We have seen examples of it used in lead generation, new product development, operational efficiency, employee engagement and brand building. There is no area of the business that cannot benefit, and there is no area of the business that will not suffer if it isn't using technology.

Find out about the Top 10 applications of AI

No matter what your business, no matter what size or what sector you are in, no matter what industry, there are new technologies arriving in droves every day that could help you create success in multiple areas of your business – and it doesn't have to be complex and you don't need a PhD to use it!

You shouldn't question if technology is applicable to your business. Rather ask how you're going to use it to differentiate your business from the competition, grow sales, improve operational efficiency, engage employees or drive product innovation.

Technology has helped level the playing field – so get scoring now!

Assimilate the very latest in technology

So how do you stay on top of what's new? Our advice is to get young people in right away to help you figure this out.

In their "Reshaping the Workplace" report, PWC said that millennials are "the first generation to enter the workplace with a better grasp of a key business tool than more senior workers."

You have to bring the insights of younger generations into your organisation and have those insights respected and listened to.

This goes beyond the traditional way of recruiting young interns to start at the bottom and work their way up the ladder.

Whether it's regular informal focus groups that tell the organisation what it doesn't want to hear, or employing a 'CTEO' – a Chief Technology Exploitation Officer – that can never be older than 30 years of age, there needs to be a respected space for a generation that uses the latest technology as part of their everyday lives.

This is not about getting rid of older generations. Some organisations now have a workforce that spans five generations. In our view, this could be incredibly valuable, especially if you have customers that span multiple generations.

Does your organisation make a point of having people from different generations in all work teams? Pairing younger and older generations often results in innovative ideas that honour the past value of the business while also building an exciting future.

It could be formal mentorship pairings, rotating shadow positions, or more informal conversations. Whatever shape it takes, you have to give your people – across all generations – opportunities to learn from AND teach others. You'll be surprised to discover how much untapped potential there is, which can help the business create exceptional products and customer experience.

We are a great example of this! Roger's experience of business and Juanita's experience in a completely different way of doing business is a firecracker combination.

Adapt the technology to make it work for you in your business

Once you're aware of the latest technology you need to see how and where it could work for your business.

Don't allow technology to disappear into a silo!

Most larger companies have silos – operations, sales and marketing, finance – and new technology can get stuck in any of them.

What you want is for every department to share their ideas on how to use one piece of technology in different ways across the entire business.

One of the reasons why smaller businesses often beat larger companies in the new technology space is simply because they don't have departmental silos and big company inertia. They can easily assimilate the new stuff, see how it might be used to advantage anywhere in the business, and move to try it out.

Adopt the technology incredibly quickly

A word of warning: no matter how up to speed you are with new technology, it is probably ancient by the time you become aware of it, or worse, already in use by your competitors. Get rid of traditional concept notes, business cases and lengthy R&D processes – take risks!

The new rules of innovation are simply get it done, make it available, listen to user feedback, and then make it better. Sometimes it's better to aim for progress over perfection.

Lastly, don't allow anyone to delay the adoption of the technology just because they've 'never done it that way before'.

Once you've gone through the assimilate, adapt, adopt process, you've got to do it all over again. Make it a habit throughout the ranks of your business so that everyone stays on the lookout for new technology that can help you win.

Exceptional companies, both now and increasingly in the future, will have mechanisms in place to welcome and motivate people from different generations that can help them assimilate, adapt and adopt new technology. These companies will have the 'what next' and 'can do' culture which together with a lack of bureaucracy allow them to be exceptionally fleet of foot.

EMPLOY EXCEPTIONAL PEOPLE

See our book Staying in the Helicopter®: The Key to Sustained Profitable Growth

Of course you need to train people, encourage them, nurture them and develop them, but you need to start with people who score 9 or 10 out of 10 throughout your organisation.

We can't be exceptional unless we have exceptional people. You cannot afford to have passengers.

Nines and tens aren't necessarily the most expensive people. They also aren't necessarily those that have been with the organisation for many years or are the most qualified. Instead, they are the people that are the absolute best fit for a specific role in your specific organisation.

People are at the very core of every organisation. In fact, it is so important that we include it here and in our book *Staying in the Helicopter®: The Key to Sustained Profitable Growth*.

In our experience, business leaders don't spend enough time on recruiting and retaining top talent. To win in the new game of business, we have to get really good at putting round pegs in round holes. Recruiting, selecting, motivating and retaining top talent is not a job that can simply be delegated to HR.

We are great believers in using every possible tool to do that, whether it is a one-day assessment centre or a custom set of online psychometric tests. These may appear to be time-consuming and costly, but it's much less expensive to use them than to recruit and train an employee who was never right for the job or whose aspirations conflicted with those of the business. The cost of getting it wrong has been estimated at something like four or even five times the employee's annual salary.

In an interview, it's often less about the answer a candidate gives than how they give that answer. Ask a few questions to get to know the person, a few that catches them off-guard, and a few to determine whether they have the depth and breadth of knowledge and experience needed for their role.

Then ask them to prove it.

Professor Jason Dana from the Yale School of Management said:

'Job interviews are useless at identifying the best candidate.'

Testing the skills of a candidate can be as simple as setting up a mock call for a potential receptionist to navigate, a prospect test for a salesperson, or a short crisis communication plan for an executive.

As part of my recruitment process, I use a battery of psychometric tests to determine whether any new employee has the behavioural characteristics that will add both harmony and value to the existing teams.

I personally write all our recruitment advertisements for every position and word it in a way that aims to weed out anything less than nines and tens. I sit in on every interview, even when the interview is led by someone else.

Candidates are also interviewed in a group format that involves everyone they will be working with regularly.

After the interview rounds, I consults with my management team, but I make the final hiring decision and ensure that the job description fits the current and future strategy of the role.

Juanita

Some time ago, I was recruiting a managing director for an Indian company and went through a one-day assessment process. After a few years I met the successful candidate, Achu Achuthan, who reminded me of the process he had gone through. 'I've never told you this before,' he said, 'but I had two other job offers, which were both more attractive than yours in terms of remuneration and prospects. But I was so impressed with the process that you went through to select me – that's the main reason why I joined you and your company. Because it seemed to me so professional and so much the right thing to do and indeed it's what I have adopted ever since in terms of recruiting people.'

Roger

Read more about this in Roger's whitepaper 'Seven Ways To Not Hire Turkeys'

BUILD HIGH PERFORMING TEAMS

As well as employing the best, we of course have to think about how we are going to get the best out of our people. You also need to think about how those people function in an organisation to be genuinely performing teams – teams that are many times the sum of their parts.

Team performance comes from four things:

1. The skills and behavioural profiles of the people in the teams
2. The direction, motivation, organisation and structure provided by the leaders of the organisation
3. The relationships within the team that are based on mutual trust, respect and support
4. The atmosphere and the culture in the team

High Performing Teams

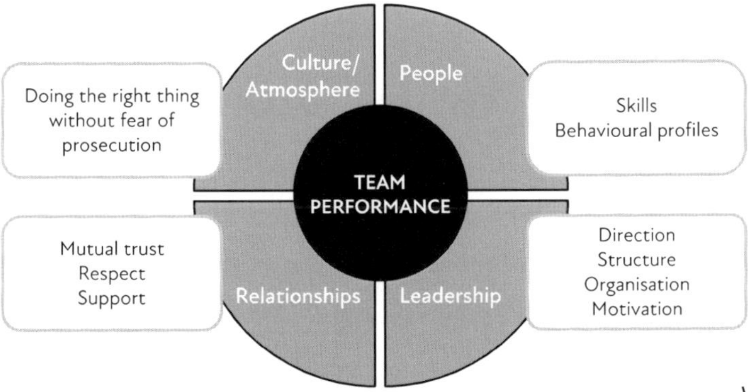

Visit the official Belbin website

Nines and tens have the skills they need to do an exceptional job. They also have the behavioural profiles that make them an asset to their teams.

Over many years of research, Professor Meredith Belbin looked at teams and the roles within the teams that people most prefer to take as well as those they least prefer. He identified nine roles:

- **Shaper:** This person is focused on the end objective like a laser beam. They aren't too fussed about how you get there, but they keep the team honest. They know where everyone is going and will not waiver. Shapers tend to be objective, challenging and dynamic people.
- **Co-ordinator:** This person is needed to clarify goals, draw out team members, and delegate work appropriately.
- **Plant:** The creative member of the team. While they are often quite difficult to manage, you need more creatives on your team than ever before. They might be unorthodox, but they're great at solving difficult problems.
- **Resource Investigator:** Most salespeople are resource investigators. They use their inquisitive nature to find opportunities and contacts outside the team to the benefit of the team.
- **Team Worker:** These are the 'people people' in the team. They're perceptive, diplomatic and cooperative, and they use these skills to help the team manage conflict. They're also very versatile and can help almost anyone on the team with their work.
- **Implementer:** These people are the opposite of team workers. They are 'tasks people'. They're practical and reliable and turn ideas into action. They can sometimes be hesitant to let go of their plans in favour of positive changes.
- **Monitor Evaluator:** Most accountants are monitor evaluators. They're logical, analytical and great at making impartial judgements. Generally, shapers and monitor evaluators don't get along. Shapers just want to get there, while monitor evaluators want to do it in small increments.
- **Completer Finisher:** Just that. Painstaking and conscientious they need to polish and perfect. They don't let the team move on until every 'i' is dotted and every 't' is crossed.
- **Specialist:** Specialists are brought in to do a very specific job. They're single-minded, self-starting and dedicated. They prefer to focus on technicalities rather than teamwork and often contribute to information overload.

One of the businesses I ran was a high-tech electronics and engineering business that used 'simultaneous engineering' to develop new products. This required a multi-disciplined group of people to work together to develop products. They had three teams running, but none of them were quite getting there. Projects seemed to always get to 80% done and then somehow all the activity dissipated.

I got fed up with this and set up an investigation. We looked at people's CVs and skill sets, as well as at the procedures they were using. This investigation revealed nothing to be concerned about. Then we used the Belbin model to evaluate the teams and discovered that, quite by chance, all three teams lacked a monitor evaluator and completer finisher. All the teams therefore got somewhere close to the finish line and then got bored.

The solution was to add a person that was comfortable in those roles to each team. It didn't matter what discipline these additional people were from. The result was that the teams – now with the addition of the missing Belbin team role – immediately started to get products out on time, every time.

Roger

Each of the nine team roles comes into play at a different stage of a task or project.

- The first person you need is the shaper to define the objective.
- Then the coordinator starts to marshal resources – both human and physical.
- Next comes the plant, the creative, ideas person, who comes up with options about how you're going to solve problems.
- Then the resource investigator starts using external contacts for the benefit of the team.
- After that you need the monitor evaluator to do all the checks and balances.
- Finally, the completer-finisher will make sure everything is tied up with a neat ribbon.

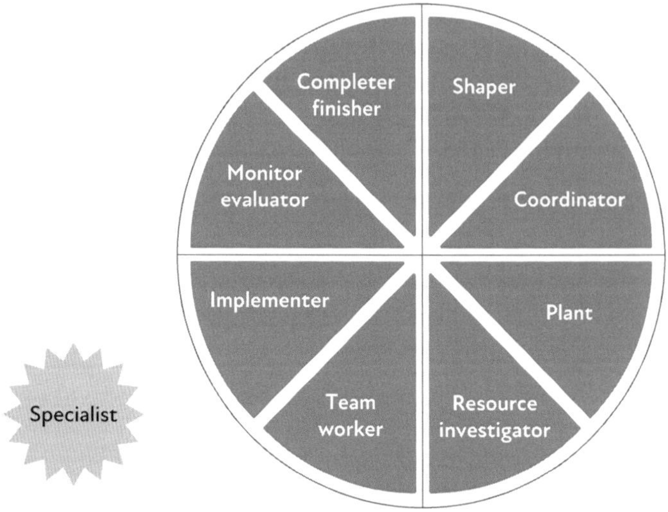

If you don't have people in that order, you'll still get the job done. It will just take twice as long.

I was a tutor for over 25 years with Europe's premier experiential leadership programme. I would spend five days with a group of eight or nine individuals who did not know each other and had been randomly selected. They would go through a series of projects – some cerebral, some physical – and they would take turns at leading and following.

During these sessions I observed over and over that it doesn't matter how skilled and experienced team members were nor how good the systems and processes in which they operate, without at least one person from each of the quadrants, the team simply will not perform.

Roger

If you want to have an exceptional business, you have to fill it with exceptional teams. There are many tools available, but Belbin is really powerful and simple to use. It wasn't designed for HR people but for those of us who actually run businesses and want to do so better and more efficiently.

FUNDAMENTAL TWO

WIN! BY BEING A GREAT PLACE TO WORK... AND PLAY

The rising trend of talent migration and emigration has triggered a war for talent. In this war, exceptional people will want to work for employers who not only value them, but whose values they share.

SHARE YOUR VALUES

The best talent has a choice these days and will simply not work for an organisation whose values they don't share.

When you're interviewing someone exceptional, it's highly likely that they're going to ask questions to help them determine whether the values of your business align with their own values. If they can't get a clear idea of what your values are or how your business practically lives those values, or they feel that their values do not align with yours, they'll go look for employment somewhere else.

The same goes for talent you already employ.

A list of values wrapped in a mission statement is simply not enough. Vision and mission statements are often designed by a committee and published on the company website without much thought on the impact those few sentences should have on everyone in the business.

The values of an organisation should be embedded in the hearts and minds of every person employed in it. Employees need to understand how to live by those values, and leaders need to consistently exhibit and promote those values.

Exceptional talent will make an exceptional contribution when their personal values align with their workplace values.

The values of many businesses were exposed for all to see through advertisements placed and policy decisions made during the 2020 COVID-19 pandemic. Some gained and some lost trust as a direct result and we believe the consequences will be long term. Values aren't fluffy hidden things: they're visible through everything your business – and everyone working in it – does.

Read more about Creating the Best Workplace on Earth

GIVE THEM WHAT THEY WANT

When workplace researchers Rob Goffee and Gareth Jones asked people about what makes 'the best workplace on earth', they identified six things:

- Identity: Let me be myself
- Transparency: Tell me what I need to know to get my job done
- Talent: Help me develop my skills
- Pride: Give me a place where I can say I'm proud to work
- Meaning: Give me work that's meaningful, not menial
- Support: Don't get in the way with stupid rules

Read more about Eight Things Your Employees Want From You

An article written by Melissa Raffoni summarises what employees want their leaders to do:

- Tell me my role, tell me what to do, and give me the rules
- Discipline my co-worker who is out of line

- Get me excited
- Don't forget to praise me
- Don't scare me
- Impress me
- Give me some autonomy
- Set me up to win

We combined this research with our own experience to create an assessment to measure whether your business is a great place to work:

- **Meaning**

  Most employees want to know why they're doing what they're doing and how it makes a difference to the business. They will go over and above what is expected of them if what they do links strongly to their values and aspirations. That's why it's so important to ask a potential hire about their values and aspirations – on top of everything else you should check – before you hire them.

  Many people also want to know how their job and employer will make a positive difference to society. We discuss this in more detail in Fundamental Four.

- **Role clarity**

  If your employees were to write down their job descriptions, would they be the same as what you and, perhaps more importantly, their immediate superior think their job descriptions are? And do they know how their responsibilities link with those of their colleagues?

  Make sure your employees know exactly what is expected of them right now. Then check in every year to see how their roles can change and grow based on the skills they learn over time. Unexpectedly great things can happen when you ask your nines and tens what they think their roles could be or could become.

- **No stupid rules**

  Yes, some of your most cherished rules might be seen a stupid by others. Stupid rules are those that haven't kept up with the times.

> I arrived at the offices of a charity organisation to be briefed for a future masterclass. The CEO and HR Director were delayed and shared that they had come from a disciplinary session in which they had to reprimand a young employee for never arriving at the office on time. When I asked if this had an impact on the person's performance the answer was: 'No, but starting at 9 o'clock is simply the way we do things.'
>
> Why?
>
> Young people don't follow rules if they don't understand the meaning behind the rules. It doesn't mean that they aren't dedicated to doing a great job.
>
> It doesn't make sense to lose your best employees over stupid rules.
>
> *Roger*

  We're not advocating for a lawless workplace or for keeping everybody happy. The 'no stupid rules' rule is about making sure you know what every rule is meant to achieve and sharing that reason with your people. Everyone gets stuck in their own ways sometimes, so ask others for their opinions on the rules and let them make suggestions for alternatives.

  Many organisations have re-evaluated their rules following the 2020 COVID-19 pandemic and the extent to which they are able to trust their people. Regular home working, for example, is now seen to be entirely possible and even more successful than purely office-based work.

- **Fair discipline**

  Employees want to see co-workers disciplined when they step out of line – they don't want soft management.

Where disciplinary action is deserved, doing nothing about it is as good as saying that you support the behaviour. A softer management style might be more comfortable but is ultimately unfair towards those staying in line.

- **Praise**

When I had just graduated my first boss was an exceptional man called Arthur Shillito. A note would often appear on my desk an hour or so after a meeting with a customer or supplier: 'Roger, thank you so much for your contribution to the meeting. I really appreciate it. Arthur.'

I was a young guy and every time I got one of Arthur's notes my shoulders would go back and my chest go out. There was nothing I wouldn't do for Arthur. It was the praise that made me feel that way, not what I was paid.

Roger

However much praise you've been giving, please give two or three times more. We're not talking just about the people down the line from you but about your peer group as well. There's absolutely nothing wrong with saying: 'That's a brilliant idea! Well done!' And why not praise your boss while you're at it? 'That was a good initiative you came up with there.' We all need praise. It's a basic human need.

Don't just wait until the regular awards ceremonies or the year-end function. Surprise people with your praise and make it special. Teach managers to do this too and to alert you when something deserves praise from 'the big boss'.

Read an article on 9 ways to praise your employees

- **Share, don't scare**

  Don't hide what's happening in the business during tough times but also don't use it to scare people into action. A good rule of thumb is to only share bad news once you are clear on exactly what needs to happen, not before.

- **Autonomy**

  Giving people autonomy doesn't mean that you're never involved in what they do. It means that you come to an agreement on what needs to be done by when and then you trust them to follow their own way to get there – obviously within the rules that keep them and the business safe and legally compliant.

  Autonomy also means that you don't turn them away when they get stuck and ask for help, but you don't micromanage them. Scheduled check-ins can help catch issues before they become costly problems, but never make these so frequent that anyone feels like you're watching over their shoulder.

  If this is making you nervous, you might need to check whether you truly have only nines and tens in your business.

I met a guy who had been a senior pilot instructor for airlines. He told me that when he started out, he wasn't that successful in teaching new pilots because he was micromanaging them. After realising that micromanaging wasn't helping, his motto became 'Experience is the sum of survivable mistakes'.

You've got to allow the people you manage to make mistakes, but you've also got to have a safety net in place for them.

Roger

Read an article on How to Share Bad News

- **Total reward**

  These days being rewarded for the work you've done is about far more than money.

  The 'Total Rewards' model developed by World at Work says that the combination of compensation, well-being, benefits, development and recognition determines how committed, inspired and productive your people will be.

- **Impress**

  Employees want to be impressed by their boss. They want to see you build on your strengths, but they also want to see you be authentic about your mistakes and personal growth.

  Employees can be the strongest 'word-of-mouth army' to spread the word and stand up for your company – but they will only do so if they're truly impressed by what their boss and the company they work for do.

- **Set up to win**

  Everyone wants to be part of a winning organisation. They want to feel proud of where they work and what they're helping to achieve.

  Make a point of sharing company successes with your people, in the media, on your website and on social media. Don't let there be a reason for any employee to ever say they're 'just' working at your organisation.

  In addition, great employees do what they can with what they have. Great places to work make sure employees have access to all the training, tools and equipment they need to create exceptional products and provide exceptional customer experience.

  That does not mean you should approve every request for new equipment or software. Sometimes it's a case of training your people how to think of

View the World at Work Total Rewards model

and use alternative ways of getting the job done. If a piece of equipment or software is absolutely crucial to them performing at their best, they should be able to convince you with strong logic. If they don't have the ability to do this, train them!

Cosatto® in the UK is on a mission to 'save the world from boring baby stuff'. Their offices reflect this focus on fun with an indoor slide, massive beanbags, gym and games.

While I was visiting them, Andrew Kluge, the CEO, told me that they were putting in a slide from the first floor to the ground floor. I asked him to explain what it was all about. Andrew said that the slide was part of a bigger project to create a work, relax and play hub in the physical centre of the business. 'We wanted to create somewhere that everyone in the company could come to chat, relax, meet, eat and generally be together.'

The slide has had an enormous effect in many respects. It has generated massive pride within the business as a whole. However bad your day is, however stressed you are – a trip down the slide just demands a smile.

The company also ensures that this spirit is reflected in various non-financial rewards for Cosatto® employees: regular chances to win prizes, monthly donations to different employee's charity of choice, monthly staff award ceremonies, and weekly fresh fruit deliveries.

Roger

Read Juanita's advice on managing a remote workforce. She's been doing it since 2011!

If you are managing a remote workforce, you might not be able to use a slide or in-office games to create a sense of community. In this case, you have to be a smart communicator to keep your people committed, inspired and productive.

If we were to come in and do a confidential survey of your employees, what would the average score for your company be on this scoring sheet?

Assessment: What Employees Want

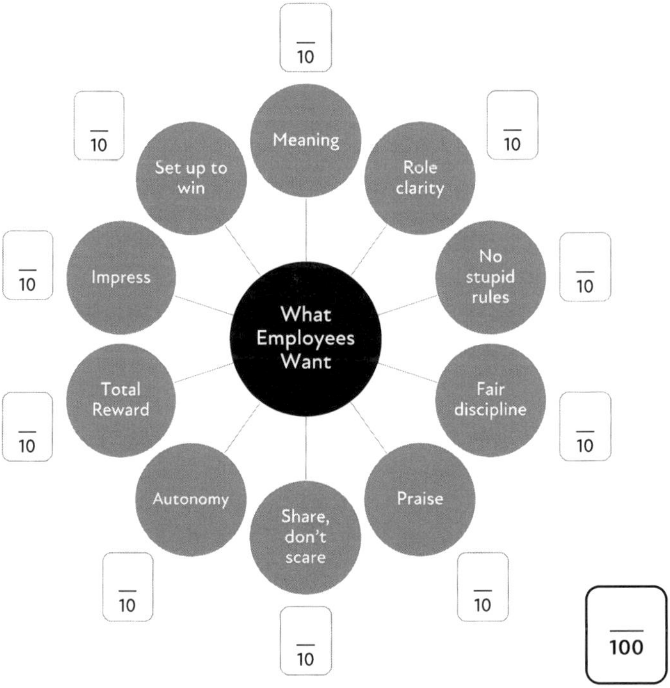

You can also complete this assessment through the app. Score each area as you think your employees would score it.

Go to our app to complete the What Employees Want assessment

What score in each area is acceptable? What score indicates that you have a culture of retaining and motivating the talent you have?

Like every area of business, it's always the dynamic that's important. Whatever you score now, it's important that when you check it again in three or six months that you have moved forward a notch or two. However, if your score is lower than 90, we suggest that you are not in the first division of exceptional.

Health Warning! It would be a great idea to actually ask your people to complete this assessment. However, please don't do so unless you are totally prepared to share – and act on – the results.

The solution doesn't have to be expensive. It's often just about better communication throughout the ranks.

The first step is to make sure that all managers are great communicators. Managers are often the most technically competent or have been with the organisation the longest, but this does not make them good managers. All managers are crucial to making your business a great place to work. Share this assessment with them and make sure they have the skills to make the necessary changes happen.

Don't leave it there, though. If you want to keep top talent, you must take personal responsibility for giving employees what they need.

FUNDAMENTAL THREE

WIN! BY CONSTANTLY PROSPECTING

It's dangerous to rely solely on existing customers.

ALWAYS BE ON THE HUNT FOR NEW CUSTOMERS

We can never simply take the risk of expecting customers to find us. This strategy may have worked for some in the past, but now it's just too dangerous, as it means you're not in full control of a very important area of your business.

Our definition of prospecting is talking to people who have never bought from you or who have not bought from you in the past couple of years.

In normal times whomever is responsible for selling in your organisation should be spending at least 20% of their time prospecting. That's one day a week. If you want to grow or are in a more testing climate, you should be spending an even bigger proportion of their time than that.

That means that if you're a sole trader you must never fill your diary with work. If you do, you won't be prospecting, and you won't have any future business. This doesn't just apply to small businesses – the same applies to businesses of all sizes across all industries.

Professional firms – lawyers, accountants, architects and, believe it or not, marketing firms – are traditionally the worst culprits.

They either seem to find the idea of 'knocking on doors' beneath them, or they fill up every possible moment with work for existing clients without making sure that there will be more projects after the current projects have been completed.

A friend of mine is a civil engineer – an expert in the design of ports. He worked for a big firm of consultants in the UK for many years and is now in his early 60s. For a long time, he said that he wanted to start passing on his knowledge to the next generation, but to no effect. Then he was approached by a major Australian firm of consultants who had a large programme of building ports to meet the demands of the China-generated boom in Western Australia. They made him an offer he couldn't refuse to move out there. They also wanted to put two young guys alongside him to learn all he knew. The position would be his swan song to what had been a rewarding career.

Not so long ago, he was back visiting the UK, and he told me something very interesting. He remarked that he had been recruited on the back of the boom and that the boom was over. China had slowed down, and there were now very few new ports under review in Australia. Imagine his surprise when he then discovered that there was no pipeline of other prospects. His large engineering consultancy that had been stacked out with work previously had stopped prospecting. They had allowed themselves to fill every minute of every day with work. Given that it takes at least 12 months for that kind of large-scale engineering project to move through the sales pipeline, the company now had a significant self-imposed challenge ahead just to survive.

While writing this book I heard that the company has now been sold to a US competitor for one dollar!

Roger

It doesn't matter what type or size of organisation you are – commercial, partnership, or not-for-profit – you have to prospect for new customers if you want to have even a chance of winning. And you can't leave the responsibility of making sure it happens to anyone else.

KEEP IT ALL ABOUT THE NUMBERS

There is a relationship between the number of properly pre-qualified leads you have in your business and the business you get. Most companies will measure that at between 5% and 20%. So, between 5% and 20% of the leads you qualify will turn into business.

What this means is that (assuming you have less than 80% market share and therefore have headroom to grow) if you double the number of leads then you will double sales.

Every business leader should have a formula to show how prospecting input affects prospecting output (sales). We need to get away from the traditional 'seat of the pants' salesperson way of doing things. If your sales team is adopting an attitude of 'let's get out there and see what we can get', they won't be as effective.

If you generate twice as many leads, you will get twice as much business. It really is as simple as that!

> When I ran the plc we felt so strongly about this we set ourselves a KPI target for 30% of annual sales to come from new customers and our performance against this was reported on monthly together with our other business KPIs.
>
> Roger

For sole traders and smaller businesses, prospecting can be a huge challenge. Doing the work that clients pay for or employing people to do this work always seems to take priority. There are many logical reasons listed by many business leaders for why sales isn't a focus.

All these reasons are, however, excuses that can be countered with this simple statement: if you don't have clients, you don't have a business.

Here is the Sales Management Matrix™, a model that we use when we work with sales forces. The Y axis indicates whether the salesperson is prospecting or not, and the X axis gives you the measure of effectiveness of your sales force: orders ahead of budget and orders behind budget. It's all pretty basic stuff.

Sales Management Matrix™

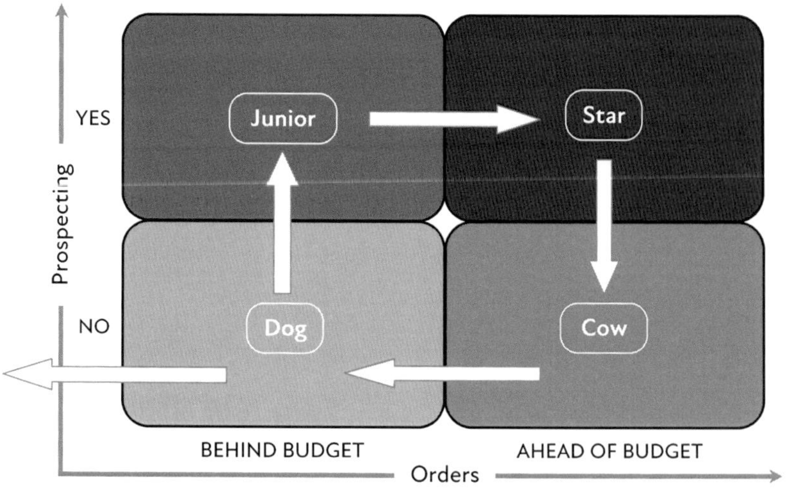

A new salesperson always starts out as a junior. By definition, they are behind budget and everything they do is prospecting. Where you find them going – where you want to have most of your salespeople – is into the star box.

Stars are ahead of budget, and they are still prospecting. So that's where you want the majority of your sales force.

It doesn't always work quite like that though, does it? Members of your sales team begin to say: 'I have too many demands placed on me by customers, and I don't really have the time to prospect anymore.' 'I'm too important to prospect.' 'I'm too busy to prospect.' They then become cash cows.

Without exception, in our experience, in every sales force, the people who are most revered aren't the stars – they're the cows. They're ahead of budget, they think they are very important, but they have stopped prospecting for whatever reason.

The cow box is, in fact, a pretty dangerous place to be. Suddenly, your second biggest customer moves to another country, the third biggest goes under, and guess what – the revered cow salesperson is behind budget and has no prospects. Then the cows turn into dogs.

There are only two choices for dogs. They can learn how to be a junior again, or they can leave the company. There is nowhere else for them to go, and you have to be brutal about this.

Rarely do we find sales managers looking at or thinking about their people – or the effectiveness of their people – in this way. The salespeople in each of the three boxes need managing in a totally different way if the business is to achieve a majority of stars. That's the vital job of sales management. No one else can do it.

Where on this model is your company's sales team?

Scan the QR code on this page to complete the Sales Management Matrix™ assessment on our app. Take this back to your sales force and ask them to complete it. Check on it regularly.

Go to our app to complete the Sales Management Matrix™ assessment

Even if you don't specifically have salespeople, you need to regularly ask yourself: 'In which of these blocks are the sales efforts of my business.'

A while ago, I was with a firm of accountants with which I'd worked before. The firm had 21 partners. The managing partner rang me up in January and asked if I'd do a masterclass for the first day of the partners' conference in spring, to which I agreed. Two or three weeks before the event, the partner rang me again and said that they had to postpone the masterclass. He asked if it would be okay if it was held on a Sunday. When I asked why, I was told that 10% of the staff had just been made redundant, and that he really didn't want them knowing that the conference was being held in a posh hotel.

So, perhaps a little mischievously, I said to the partner: 'With 10% redundancies, presumably that means there are only going to be 19 partners from now on?' 'Oh no,' the partner said, 'it doesn't really work like that – the partners aren't affected.' At this point, I decided I was really going to go for these guys when my day with them came around. I hadn't been planning to show them the sales management matrix model, but I was getting so frustrated with what they were saying to me.

On the day of the masterclass, I put up the sales matrix slide and asked them to tell me where the centre of gravity of the partnership was. And guess what? All 21 partners, who owned the business, said that they were cow moving to dog. I asked: 'So what are you going to do about it?' They all shrugged their shoulders and said: 'Probably nothing.'

I really thought that I had trained myself to not get emotionally involved with clients, but that night I drove home with white knuckles on my steering wheel. I couldn't help thinking: 'There are going to be a lot more people losing their jobs because of their incompetent management.'

It's irresponsible! A level of arrogance that says: 'New clients will find us.'

Roger

RESEARCH PROSPECTS BEFORE MAKING CONTACT

It is always staggering to see how many salespeople don't use the easily accessible tool that is social media before they go out and meet a prospect. You can turn a cold lead into a warm lead just by, for example, finding out which sports team they support.

This applies to all of us – before you talk to someone you've never met before, adopt the discipline of checking them out on LinkedIn or other social networks. Do a quick Google search to find a recent article they wrote or contribution they made. Prospects love it when they see that you've made an effort to prepare for a meeting.

I remember being caught in a sales meeting where the salesperson was obviously very ill prepared. Right from the start, he launched straight into a non-stop explanation of what his company did, how great they were, what they've achieved, and how important it was that I buy from them.

It turned out that he didn't know in which position I was employed at that time, and that the position had absolutely no relevance to his sales pitch.

Even worse, the product being sold was a piece of manufacturing equipment that had nothing to do with the skills development services my employer at the time offered. The only connection between the two was one word in the company's name.

The salesperson had based the entire meeting on his assumptions, not on checking out the prospect. Needless to say, no sale was made that day.

Juanita

PITCH TO WIN

These days about 85% of the buying decision is taken online. (See more on this in the Discovery/Purchase Process model included in our book *Staying in the Helicopter®: The Key to Sustained Profitable Growth.*) The last 15% of the decision is increasingly being made during face-to-face pitching, which is often the first – and only – time you'll get to see the client face-to-face.

It's a specific skill, and most of us do it wrong.

An effective pitch needs to have been planned like a military operation and get three things perfect.

- **Structure:** The shape of exactly what it is you're going to say and how you're going to say it.

  The number one mistake we see during sales pitches is that it's all about the seller, not the buyer.

  Researchers show that attention retention in a typical 20- to 30-minute presentation reaches its maximum five minutes in. At that point your audience subconsciously decides whether they're interested or not. From there on, how much attention they pay and what they remember will automatically decline – even if they are interested.

  This means that right on the five-minute mark you should very succinctly be talking about the benefits of your solution to their problem, not about the history of your company (as we often see happen).

  Make it less about you and more about them by following this structure:

  - Start with a quick introduction that includes asking a question to check whether the requirements you built the pitch are still the same. You'll be surprised how often these have changed! If it has changed, you obviously have to think fast to work the new requirements into your pitch.

See our book Staying in the Helicopter®: The Key to Sustained Profitable Growth

- Then, right on that all-important five-minute mark, explain succinctly how your solution is going to solve their problem. If you've done a good job so far, they'll be interested in hearing the rest of the pitch.
- Only then do you do some justification that includes a little bit about your company. Doing this after explaining your solution builds credibility and trust in your solution.
- Then, you briefly repeat the benefits again before you do a trial close – but don't ask for the order. What you do instead is ask: "Does this seem interesting so far?" They may well say that your solution is exactly what they want and then you've got the order. But if they don't, you've got a bit more work to do.
- The questions and answers bit comes next, and if they're interested, you might be in the room longer than expected.
- Your last question before you leave the room should be for the order. It seems obvious, but a pitch without a close that asks for an order is just a chat. If you have a sales team that takes care of pitching, make sure they never leave without asking for the order.

Timeline of an Effective Pitch

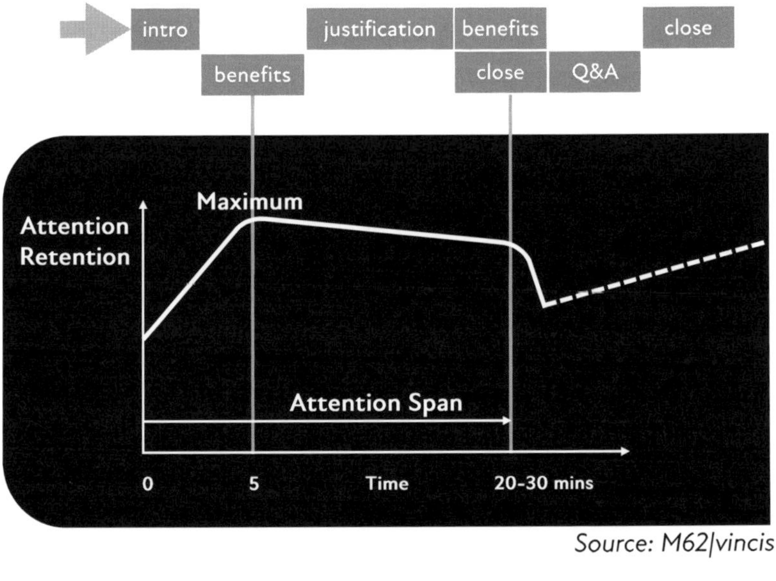

Source: M62|vincis

- **Delivery:** Who's going to make the pitch.

  There are few things worse than having to sit through a pitch where two or even three people try to pitch as a team, but they have obviously not rehearsed beforehand. It just makes the company seem unprofessional.

  Even if you're pitching alone, rehearse! Be absolutely clear on what it is you want to say, about what, at what time. Put in the time and effort!

- **Design:** The slide deck and any other supporting materials or samples.

  If you do use slides, never, ever have more than 16 words on a slide and never read them word for word – your audience can do that themselves!

  The slides are not there as a crib sheet for you, they're meant to be visual support for what you're saying. However many slides you have, cut them by half. You don't need as many as you think, and it's never more than one slide for every three minutes of presentation time.

  If you get the structure, delivery and design right, then it's generally recognised that your success rate will improve by at least 20%.

Effective Pitch

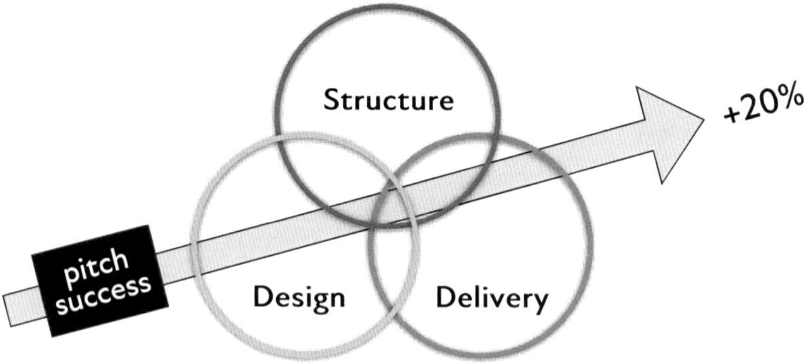

I once ran a Present & Pitch for Profit masterclass for the entire salesforce and top team of a £200 million manufacturing company. At the end, the CEO did some calculations and said: 'Roger, I am quite convinced that as a result of what we have learnt on pitching, it will directly add £8 million at least to our top line next year!'

Roger

Never assume that your salespeople are great at selling face-to-face. Test them and train them until they're highly skilled at moving buyers from a 'no' to a 'yes'.

Of course, you and your salespeople have to know the solution inside out and have great sales skills – but a successful pitch needs more. Without enthusiasm and belief, you might as well not show up to pitch.

You've got to be excited about your solution and believe in it, otherwise you'll never be able to convince anyone to buy from you.

SELL TO PEOPLE WHO HAVE MONEY

The golden rule of business is to sell to people who have money! It applies to every single one of us.

It may seem obvious, but you'd be surprised how many people we've met who have been trying to sell the same things to the same people for years irrespective of the economic shifts triggered by recessions or the 2020 pandemic. Trying to sell to people who can't afford a product or service will simply never work.

Watch this to check if you are using the six factors of influence in all your marketing and sales efforts

I met a guy in Northampton, UK, who had a building company and I asked how business was. The owner said: 'Fabulous!' When I questioned further, the owner told me that back in 2008 when the recession hit, the company had nothing. All their business disappeared. The owner then told me that he and his partner got into their helicopter (see our book *Staying in the Helicopter®: The Key to Sustained Profitable Growth*) and asked: 'Who's got money?'

Now the only building work they do is extensions to London properties that are worth more than £5 million. He said: 'Of course, I have to wear a tie now and we have a glossy brochure. But we're making more money than you can imagine, with margins that are nothing short of phenomenal.'

Roger

See our list of industry ups and downs caused by the COVID-19 pandemic

KEEP AN EYE ON GLOBAL TRENDS

As well as selling to people who have money, you also have to keep in mind that money moves. It happened during the COVID-19 pandemic, and it will happen again over the coming decades as global trends create new market needs.

Access the details of the Roland Berger Trend Compendium

On the following pages are some of the 2030 key trends predicted by Roland Berger Strategy Consultants.

If any of these global trends or emerging countries hold an opportunity for you, get in there! You need to stay on top of this to WIN! in this new game of business.

MEGATREND	SUBTREND	2030 CHANGE	OPPORTUNITIES
Demographics	Population location	Majority of population growth in developing countries	Basic resources
	Aging	50% of the world's population older than 33	Products and services for 60+ generation
	Urbanisation	Megacities in developing countries	Infrastructure development
Globalisation	BRICS and beyond	Increased growth in Brazil, Russia, India, China and South Africa	Establish presence in new emerging markets
Resources	Energy	Increased demand for energy in emerging markets	Energy efficiency improvements and alternative energy generation and storage
	Water and food	Increased pressure on water and food supplies	Reduce water use in production processes
Climate change	Global warming	More frequent and intense extreme weather events	Change operations to mitigate climate change
	Ecosystems at risk	Loss of 33% of terrestrial biodiversity and 60% of coral reefs	New business opportunities in response to climate change

MEGATREND	SUBTREND	2030 CHANGE	OPPORTUNITIES
Technology	Life sciences	Increase in contagious, age-related, and pollution-related diseases	Technology to enable remote medical services
	Digital transformation	Critical-mass adoption of Industry 4.0 technologies	Adapt business model to be fully digital
Knowledge	Knowledge	Global rise in education enrolment and completion rates	Invest in primary education infrastructure and 'learn anytime, anywhere' higher education
	War for talent	Digital transformation demands better educated people	Attract students from developing markets
Responsibility	Society	Demand for reporting on corporate social responsibility	Strategic partnerships between NGOs and private companies
	Businesses	Philanthropic responsibilities as a given	Replace resource exploitation through innovation

FUNDAMENTAL FOUR

WIN! BY FOCUSING ON THE SCORE – THE TRIPLE BOTTOM LINE

No business can achieve its objectives unless it generates a profit that can be reinvested in part or in whole into the business. In the new game of business, that profit should not be at the expense of people or the planet.

PASSION ALONE CAN'T SUSTAIN A BUSINESS

While passion is a key ingredient of any successful business or charity, it can never replace the need for profitability if we wish to grow.

Every business needs to focus on its sustained profitable growth.

When we work with businesses to help them focus on their sustained growth, we often start off by asking them about their purpose – why they exist and what success means to them (see our book *Staying in the Helicopter®: The Key to Sustained Profitable Growth*).

When we work with charities and member associations we find that it's easier for them to lose sight of the profitability of the organisation. Not-for-profit is, in fact, a total misnomer. The term should really be not-for-profit-*distribution*. Most need to generate profits to reinvest in the organisation in order to grow it and be able to do more for their beneficiaries.

I once worked with a firm of architects. There were six shareholders, four of whom were on the board and two of whom were managers. I had the top team of 14 directors and managers in the room.

So I asked my usual question: 'What's the purpose of the business? What is it there for?'

On the flip chart, I wrote down whatever they said, and I got all kinds of answers like: 'We want to be the best architects in the world,' and, 'We want to save the planet.' So it went on and on and on.

As I was getting close to the end of the second page on the flip chart a small voice spoke up. The lady who did the internal administration said: 'I'm a shareholder in this business and I'd quite like a return that's better than putting my money in a bank.' There was total silence in the room and then the CEO, unbelievably, said: 'We've never thought about that before!'

They then spent the rest of the day and a half's training session talking about what being in business really meant.

The CEO rang me later and told me what a huge turning point that moment had been for the business.

Roger

USE A SIMPLE MEASURE OF GROWTH

When Roger first started in manufacturing, there existed a great long formula to measure something called productivity. It involved various people like rate fixers, time-and-motion clerks, and all sorts of considerations that barely exist now. In fact, not many people talk about productivity these days, but we really ought to. There is one really simple key performance indicator (KPI) that you should be using all the time:

$$\frac{\textit{gross margin}}{\textit{number of people}} = \$/£/€/R$$

If you set a target to improve that by 10% every single year, you will never look back. You will fly. If you have a big range of salaries, you might use sales/unit cost of payroll. The important thing is that you stick with the same formula, that it's simple, that everyone in your business understands it, and that the trend keeps moving in line with your set target.

This should be a prime KPI for your business and appear on your monthly report.

GET TO NEW LEVELS OF SALES

As we explored in the previous chapter, there is a direct relationship between the amount of time your salespeople spend professionally prospecting and the business you get. If you can double the time they spend selling to pre-qualified leads, you will double your business. It really is that simple!

A study by Pace Productivity looked at how most field salespeople spend their time. According to the study, salespeople spend 6% of their time prospecting, which we've already mentioned is not enough. They spend 22% of their time servicing the customer and 23% actively selling. Then there's a massive 50% of their time that they spend on travel and administration.

See details of the Pace Productivity research

Salesperson's Time

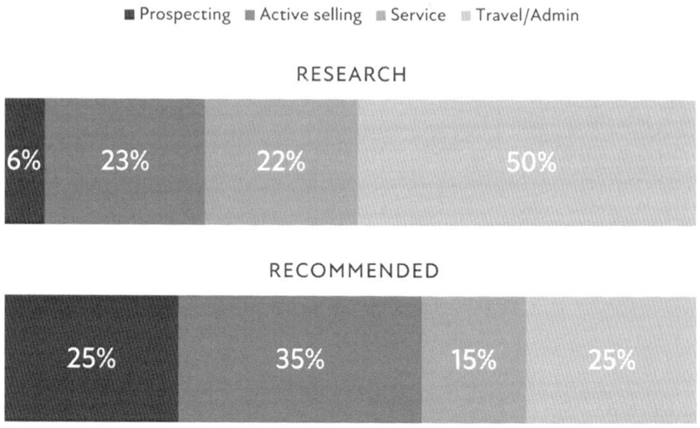

What that means is that the typical salesperson is only spending a third of their time doing what you pay them to do. Is this what it ought to be?

We've already said they should be spending at least 20% of their time prospecting. Let's say 25%. Let's change the time they spend actively selling to 35%, leave 15% of their time for service, because you can't really get away from that. Then they should spend no more than 25% on travel and admin.

If you can achieve that, you will simply double the time they spend sitting in front of properly pre-qualified leads and the consequence can only be that you double sales!

Unfortunately, not many management teams think like this.

So how do you actually achieve this? Even when your sales team is office based and don't visit customers in person, the same philosophy still applies. What is needed is a combination of training and technology.

Have you ever asked your salespeople – and by that we mean anyone who ever asks a customer for an order – whether they have received any basic sales training? We often find that those expected to sell have never been properly trained. We feel so strongly about sales training that we recommend that everyone in your company who ever talks to any customer for any reason – including credit control, for example – receive training in basic sales skills.

Next on the list is understanding the role technology can play in the sales process. We still come across companies where managers say: 'We don't give our salespeople laptops or tablets, they might lose them,' or, 'We haven't got a CRM (customer relationship management) system because it costs too much money.' Salespeople must first do their homework before visiting a prospective customer. They need to establish the probability of success (i.e. the lead turning into an order) for each prospect and should not be going out the door unless there is a more than 50% chance of getting the business.

It is an absolute necessity that all this information be stored in a central place accessible to all relevant people in the organisation. This central accessibility both reduces the risk to your business when salespeople leave and increases the opportunities to delight customers with a personal touch.

You need a proper CRM system on which salespeople can report back. CRMs don't need to be expensive, but they are only effective if there is the strongly enforced discipline that **every** contact with the client or customer by anyone in the organisation (including you!) goes into the system.

If your company already has a CRM system you need to go and check whether the right type of information is captured by the sales team and whether the CRM system actually helps the salespeople to perform better.

I worked with a company that manufactured and distributed agriculture products. The company had, a year earlier, implemented a CRM system with an app that allowed the salespeople to log details about their customer visits from wherever they were.

The management team reported that the salespeople were quite resistant to using the new system due to a variety of reasons, many of which had been quickly fixed by the system provider during the initial implementation period. However, the list of reasons for not using the CRM in the way it was designed kept on growing.

So I asked the management team whether they had consulted the salespeople during the system design process and whether use of the system was connected to performance reviews. The answer to both questions was no.

A great CRM system has to make it easy for salespeople to enter information on customer interaction without increasing the amount of time they spend on admin. It should also provide you with reports that highlight areas of the sales function that might need more discipline.

Juanita

KNOW YOUR BUYER'S GAME

Every buyer in the world has a job to do. Part of that job is to try to turn your product or service into a commodity. Their goal is to find what you have to offer for dirt cheap and without having to build a relationship with you. If they could replace you with an online auction, they would!

You have to assume that any buyer is highly trained and knows how to play the game of getting the best price.

It is your job – and the job of your salespeople – to do exactly the opposite. You have to turn their perception of what you're selling from something that even the lowest bidder can give them into something of high added value that they can only get from you.

Price/Perception Matrix™

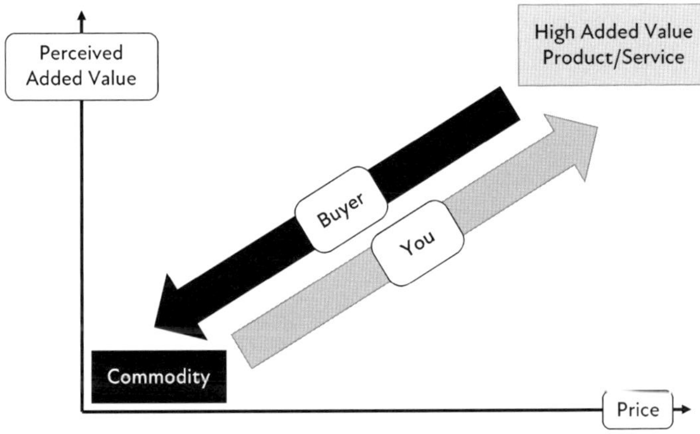

In the list of reasons of why customers buy your product, price must be lower than number 3. Write this into your salespeople's contracts and never give salespeople price discretion. They'll hate it, because selling on perceived value is much harder than selling on price, but it will keep their focus on their role in building the bottom line.

Remember, you're putting massive investment into creating added value, and it's their job to sell it. That's what they're there for.

In harder economic times, buyers feel they have more power – so you have to know how to respond when buyers play hardball.

Always remember that the moment you discount, you're saying that your value is less.

If you really have to do something, then give them 'stuff'. If you run a car dealership, give a year's worth of monthly car washes for free. If you run a professional services company give a few reports or meetings for free. Give 'stuff' that costs you very little or nothing but that has a high perceived value to them.

If you really do believe you have to give a discount, please only do it in return for something that is not just the order. It might be some video testimonials, it might be referrals, but the thinking must be that our price is what it is because of the value we give. That's our price and we mean it.

A Vistage Chair rang me up with some feedback from a recent masterclass. Two of the delegates were co-owners of a company, and shortly after the masterclass, they had an enquiry from one of their existing customers. Traditionally, this particular customer was always given a 20% discount.

With this enquiry they remembered what I had said about discounting and they decided on 'stuff' to give the customer. The deal was sealed – with no discount. It works!

Roger

Everyone buys irrationally, no matter what they're buying. It's all about perception and we can change perceptions. Whether we are in business-to-consumer or in business-to-business, the same applies.

Running a business is about taking risks and the risks associated with sticking to prices that reflect your value is small. Above all, remember that your hard work deserves higher prices!

FOCUS ON OPERATIONAL EFFICIENCY AND THE BOTTOM LINE

It's not just about your salespeople and how they are spending their time. What about the rest of the people in the organisation?

Focus on how you maximise the time everyone in your organisation spends on doing what only they can do.

It's our job as business leaders to enable people to do their job and to make sure they are doing the job only they can do.

A client of mine was a firm of land surveyors who weren't making any money. They had a full order book – and in that industry they charge by the hour. They kept recruiting more and more surveyors, but surprisingly nothing much happened to the bottom line.

I asked them what their bill/book ratio was – the hours billed to clients as a percentage of the total hours available – and they didn't know. So I helped them work it out for the previous year and it was below 30%. No wonder the business wasn't making any money!

What they found was that each surveyor really did what they wanted with no standardisation of paperwork and no thought as to how they spent their highly qualified time. So I started with the senior surveyors and worked down through the organisation with the focus wholly on maximising the time they spent doing what only they could do. It took just over a year for the bill/book ratio to move closer to 70%. Just imagine what that did to the bottom line! All that was needed was to get everyone disciplined and make sure that the firm had the right people doing the right job focussed on the bottom line.

Roger

If you have someone qualified to do something, then that's what that person should spend the majority of their time doing. It may be common sense, but very few of us think like that.

While working with a member association, I discovered that the CEO was heavily involved in tedious administrative issues. While the organisation had enough staff and skills on board, the culture of the organisation was one of always helping anyone that needed a hand.

This type of organisational culture seems highly desirable but often has the flip side of specialised staff not focusing enough on what they were hired to do.

After a tough heart-to-heart I had with the CEO, she made a number of changes and soon reported that she was able to get to more of the duties she had been hired for – without having to put in as many overtime hours.

Juanita

You can increase operational efficiency by making sure everybody understands what role they play in contributing to the top line and in driving costs down.

It's our experience that if you set your mind to drive your costs down by 10%, you probably will. You just have to decide that you are going to – and it has to come from the top. It won't happen otherwise, and it's easier to do than you think.

You should assume that everything is negotiable. We believe in putting every supplier through a beauty parade every three years – even the auditors. Everyone hates the amount of work that goes along with it, but it always results in massive reductions to overheads. You can do the same, you just need to make up your mind to do it.

Here, we're not talking about unfair business where you demand to get more than you pay for. It is more about reviewing whether the product or service still aligns with the needs of the business. There is no sense in paying for services out of habit or loyalty.

I had an engineering company client who won a contract worth £1.6 million. It just so happened that I was actually sitting in the company owner's office when a phone call came through from the customer saying they wanted to see him the next day to have the final discussions. I then asked the owner to call the managing director of their largest supplier – a company in Yorkshire that would provide electrical equipment to the value of about £580 000 for the contract – and use these words:

'I've just been told by a major new customer that we'll be awarded an important contract tomorrow if we can sharpen our pencil. I'm prepared to commit to you that if I get the contract, you will get the contract from me. What can you do on the price?'

He was immediately given a 10% reduction on the supplier's quote. That's £58 000 straight on the bottom line.

After that, they went through the next five suppliers and the average reduction he got, just by asking, was around 7%.

Roger

You need to assume that everything's negotiable. If you don't ask, you don't get.

Now we have to talk about the two most dangerous words known to business: quantity discounting. Let's say you have a 30% gross margin business. If you put your prices down by 10% and you want the profit to stay exactly the same, how much more volume do you need to stand still? The most common answer is 20%. The mathematically correct answer is 50%!

But, of course, it isn't 50% in reality. Because if you have 50% more volume going through the business, you'll probably have to pay overtime and perhaps you'll have to rent a warehouse or take on some other expense. You probably need nearer 60-70% more volume – and all just to stay exactly where you were before you discounted.

The easiest thing to be in business is a busy fool!

The other side of the coin is what happens when you put your prices up by 10%? Again, keeping profit exactly the same, how many customers can you afford to lose?

The maths here say 25%. Maybe you can lose those bad payers and some of those difficult customers. That would make for an overall healthier business.

> I used to work for BTR, which was one of the biggest corporations in the UK. If you were running one of their units, as I was, you were invited to London every year to meet with the CEO, Sir Owen Green, for a four-hour forensic examination of your budget.
>
> I remember well that I would sometimes have my hand on the door ready to leave at the end of the meeting when a little smile would appear on Sir Owen's lips and he'd say: 'Just one more thing... what would happen if you put your prices up by 1% at 9 o'clock tomorrow morning?'
>
> Of course I would say: 'Not a lot, I suppose.' and Sir Owen would say: 'Well, we'll do that then, shall we?'
>
> *Roger*

That's a fair question for anyone in business, and for you. What would happen if you put your prices up by 1% tomorrow morning at 9 o'clock? Remember, there's something about price that doesn't apply to anything else. It goes straight on the bottom line to reinvest in the growth of your business.

In our experience, most of us undervalue ourselves, and particularly those of us running small businesses. It's time we stopped!

If you're having doubts, think about this: we know that supermarkets, for example, vary. In South Africa we are likely to find cheaper prices at Pick n Pay or Checkers. So why is it that Woolworths does so well? We know, as we walk in the door of Woolworths, that we are going to pay more for the same basket of shopping. So why do we do it? We go there because of the status connected to it, and the customer experience they have developed for us.

Supermarkets driven by price alone – like Pick n Pay or Checkers – have to be driven by operational excellence and run their businesses with that driver at the fore.

There's much more on this in our book *Staying in the Helicopter®: The Key to Sustained Profitable Growth*.

See our book Staying in the Helicopter®: The Key to Sustained Profitable Growth

Like Woolworths, however, most of us are in the business of 'perceived added value', and that means we need to be charging premium prices for whatever it is we do and particularly for the relationship we have with our customers.

The attitude you need to have throughout your entire organisation is one of being proud to be doing an outstanding job – and it needs to reflect in your pricing.

If you are driven by Customer Intimacy or Product Leadership (more on this in our book *Staying in the Helicopter®: The Key to Sustained Profitable Growth*), it's the job of you and your salespeople to turn the perception of whatever it is you're selling into a higher value-added product or service.

COUNT MORE THAN JUST THE MONEY

These days, each of us running a business or involved in running a business has the additional responsibility of treating the planet and its people with respect. Your business can become the best *in* the world as well as be the best *for* the world – generally known as the 'triple bottom line'.

An increasing number of customers and investors want to spend their money with companies that take responsibility for reducing any negative impact they have on the environment or the well-being of people.

Society expects businesses to not only take care of employees but also protect the rights of those that have an indirect hand in helping you make a profit. Sole traders and small businesses have started using social media to call out clients that don't pay the agreed amounts on time, and public backlash against factories that violate labour laws or use processes that put people in harm's way have already forced many businesses to find better ways.

Taking responsibility for the triple bottom line of profit, planet and people is not just an obligation – it can be a great opportunity!

Global market research company Nielsen says that the US market for sustainable products will reach $150 billion within a couple of years. They've also found that almost half of surveyed global consumers said they would be willing to forgo a brand name in order to buy environmentally friendly products.

Read Nielsen's advice on the 6 simple guidelines for sustainability in the context of today.

Ice cream manufacturers Ben & Jerry's use nothing but fair trade, GMO-free ingredients. Their employee benefits are praised for promoting equality, and they've developed a dairy farm sustainability program in their home state of Vermont in the US. And they keep on turning a steady profit!

Even small changes, like switching off the lights in unused areas, can reduce the environmental impact of your business – it can also reduce expenses and even help increase income over time!

Consumers and governments are becoming more educated about the impact of businesses that make their profit at the expense of the planet or people. It's already highly visible in the fast-moving consumer goods (FMCG) sector, and it's gaining momentum everywhere else.

You've got to know what the impact is of everything that comes into your business and everything that comes out of your business – and you've got to take responsibility for making it better.

If you depend on assembly lines, make sure the people working on those lines are paid and treated fairly.

If you're in manufacturing, it might mean sourcing your raw materials responsibly, designing alternatives that reduce emissions, or dealing with waste more responsibly.

I visited an environmental solutions company whose mission is to reduce the waste sent to landfill. During my tour of the recycling plant and talks with the managing director, I discovered how big an impact the marketing department of any business has on the landfill problem.

Too few marketing departments understand how their labelling decisions can determine whether packaging is recyclable or not. Furthermore, using recyclable plastic for the packaging but sticking a non-recyclable label with glue to the packaging makes the entire item unrecyclable.

Trademark packaging is also an issue. The tiniest flaw in a run of trademark-shaped packaging material gets it rejected. If packaging producers don't have partnerships with companies like the one I visited, hundreds of thousands of brand-new bottles, jars and boxes go straight to landfill!

Juanita

Make the changes you need to make. You can do it yourself or partner with a specialist or non-profit organisation that can help you do it – and then tell your customers what you've done.

Showing that you are aware of your business being part of – and responsible for – society is increasingly important.

The Langham, the oldest five-star hotel in London, did this when they celebrated their 155th birthday by rewarding London's key workers during the COVID-19 pandemic with a '24-Hour Virtual Afternoon Tea Party'. They delivered afternoon tea and a surprise overnight stay voucher to NHS teams, emergency services, TFL staff, taxi drivers and many other key workers.

Make these socially responsible efforts a consistent part of your business – and be genuine about it. Social media users are quick and harsh in calling companies out for greenwashing or publicity stunts.

Have a look at what The Langham did

You have no choice. Over the next decade more and more people will buy from companies that are winning in the new game of business with respect for the planet and its people.

THE SHAPE OF WINNING ORGANISATIONS

SO WHAT'S THE 'shape' of a winning organisation in this game of business?

Firstly, you've got to be agile. You've got new technology arriving at eye-watering speed. You've got new markets appearing all the time – you simply have to be fleet of foot. This is where smaller businesses often have the edge on larger ones that tend to have an inertia that holds them back.

To be agile, you need to take advice from and listen to younger generations, and you need to get rid of silos in your business.

People are expensive: you need talent throughout and truly performing teams that are more than the sum of their parts.

You need to be an adaptive leader. Adaptive leaders are people who are always looking over the horizon expecting change. They cannot spell the word status quo, and they're always *Staying in the Helicopter*®.

If you're running a business or are involved in running a business, you need to spend at least 20% of your time in your helicopter focussed on the four fundamentals of business. That's a day a week. You've got to find a way to do that. It might be by delegating better, by trusting others more, by better time management, or maybe by getting rid of unnecessary structures and procedures.

If you are not up in that helicopter looking over the horizon, nobody else will.

Finally, you need a culture of innovation throughout the organisation. You need to empower everyone to come up with new ideas, whatever they may be, and to be listened to. You want the whole organisation feeding into the opportunities made possible by new technology.

Winning Organisations

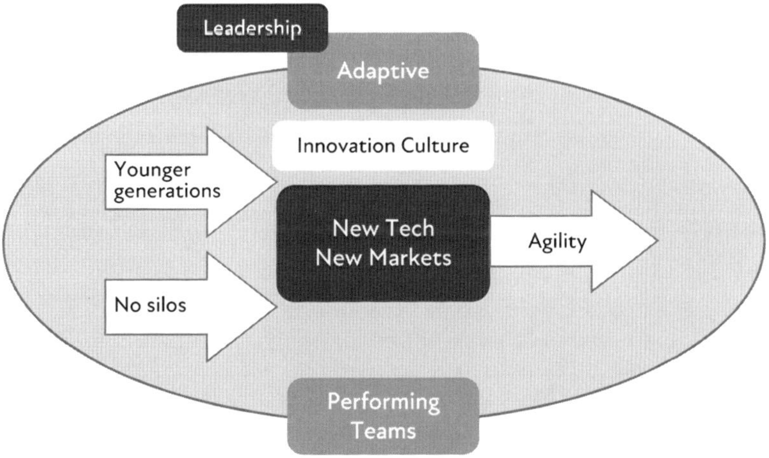

Above all, remember as a leader you need to exhibit ***Belief, Passion*** and ***Courage***.

YOUR GAME PLAN

SO THAT'S THE four fundamentals of business. If you were to do an assessment on your business now, how would you rate out of 100? What score would let you sleep at night? 85? 90? Whatever it is, once again, it's the dynamic that's important – that you are always moving forward.

Complete your scores now and then check again in three months and again in six months. Doing this in our app will make it easy to keep track.

The trend needs to be upwards if you are to continue winning in this new game of business. Maybe you could have each of your employees complete it – but, once again, please remember you have to be prepared to share the results and take action on any areas highlighted for improvement.

Go to our app to complete the Fundamentals of Business assessment

Fundamentals of Business

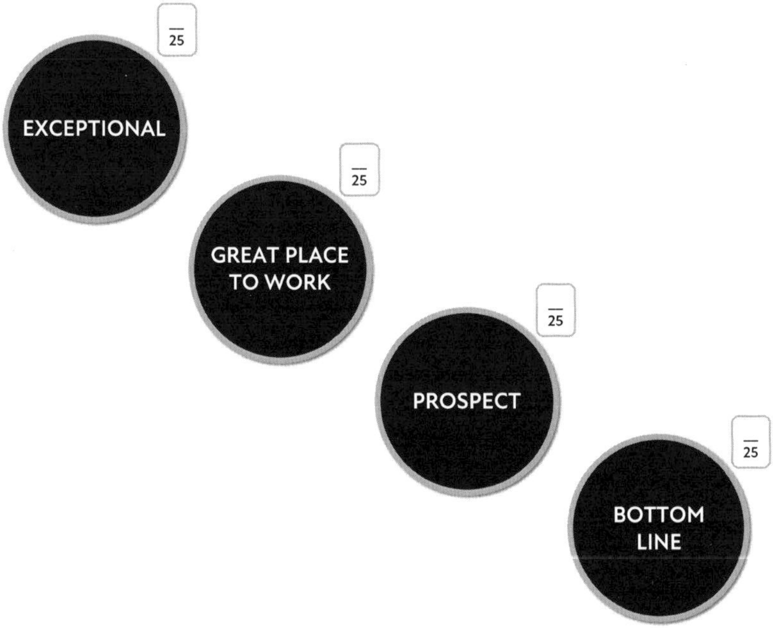

TOTAL SCORE OUT OF 100

WHAT SCORE WILL LET YOU SLEEP AT NIGHT?

STAY IN TOUCH WITH US

Roger Harrop
roger@rogerharrop.com
www.rogerharrop.com

Juanita Vorster
juanita@juanitavorster.com
www.juanitavorster.com

Book us for keynote speeches and masterclasses on these topics, each tailored to your needs and ideal outcomes:

- Staying in the Helicopter®: The Key to Sustained Profitable Growth
- WIN! How to Succeed in the New Game of Business
- Electrify Your Profitability™
- Sparkling Sales – In Good Times or Bad
- Effective Leadership Today
- Creativity, Technology, Speed and Change
- Present & Pitch for Profit

www.theceoexperts.com